by:

Sara Slavin

and

Deborah Jones

photographs:

Deborah Jones

art direction & styling:

Sara Slavin

text:

Linda Peterson

design:

Morla Design

First published 1996 by
Collins Publishers San Francisco
1160 Battery Street,
San Francisco, California 94111
HarperCollins Web Site:
http://www.harpercollins.com

Book and Cover Design: Morla Design
Food Styling: Sandra Cook
Photo Assistants: Jeri Jones,
Sara Gummere, Virginia deCarvalho,
and Ellen Callaway

Library of Congress Cataloging-in-Publication Data:
Slavin, Sara. Linens: elements of the table /
by Sara Slavin: photography by Deborah Jones.
p. cm.
ISBN 0-00-225083-7
1. Table setting and decoration.
2. Household linens. I. Title.
TX879.S58 1996
642'.7--dc20   96-15434
                        CIP

Printed in China
10 9 8 7 6 5 4 3 2 1

contents:

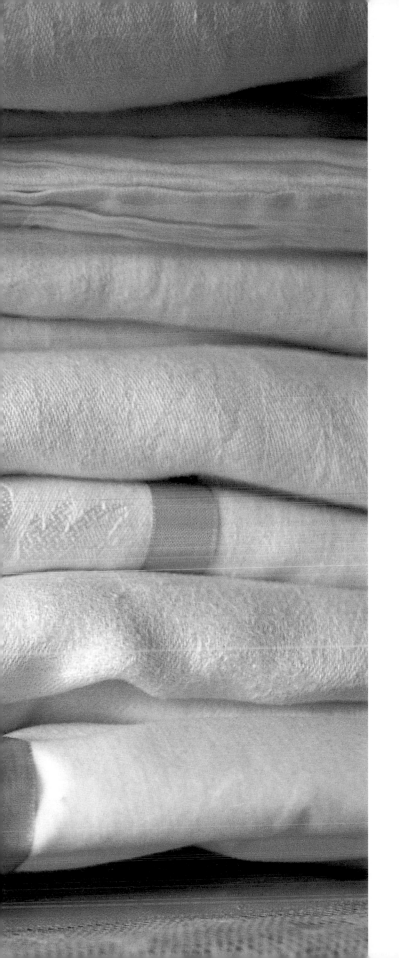

treasured

Once upon a time, brides established their linen closets with the contents of the trousseau. The word originally meant a little trusse or bundle that the fresh young bride carried with her to her husband's home. It was part of the bride's "riches." She brought both her own personal linens and household linens with her to begin her home.

Today, households are formed, dissolved, and reformed in any number of ways. Those who care about the table may haunt tag sales, catalogs, and fabric stores, or (if they're lucky) rummage in a mother's or grandmother's linen closet for treasures. ∽

This book is for linen lovers — people who appreciate the many ways tablecloths, napkins, runners, and their kin add to the enjoyment of domestic life. In this chapter you'll find a little history and lore about linens, and a few stories that remind us of why we hold simple squares, circles, or rectangles of cloth so dear. There are also tips from the trade on keeping linens, old and new, looking fresh, as well as some hints on shopping for vintage linens.

the art of the cloth

For domestic sensualists, the Dutch still-life paintings of the 17th century are all about table-cloths. We are linen lovers, and we see the objects of our affection, no matter where they are hidden. We see beyond the warm, butter-yellow light the painters created, underneath the faithfully rendered fruit and cheese and fish and fowl. We see the table linens — light and shadow-sculpted, creamy, textured, or delicately lace-edged — and we want to touch. In these paintings, as in our lives, the linens are the canvas on which the tabletop art of domestic life is created. Before the cutlery, before the glasses, before the meal, comes the linen. It can be soft cotton, washed so many times that the very feel of the worn cloth is a touch as comforting as home. It can be rich damask, its elegant surface catching and reflecting light so that by sunlight or candles, you see the elegant tracery of the weave. ◡

color

The use of color in linen, a phenomenon we take for granted today, is actually a rather modern development. Marc Porthault, whose family founded the great French linen firm that bears his name, credits his mother with the innovation. Madeleine Porthault fell in love with the delicate hues inspired by the natural botanical world, and with the changing lights of the seasons. From the delicate hue of champagne to the richer, deeper colors of cornflowers and marigolds, color now adds an additional dimension to table linens. ⌢

An appreciation for linen has its origin in respect for the function of the beautiful. Domestic life is enriched by objects that are not only useful but stimulating to the imagination as well.

Whatever restrictive rules once existed about "matching" have disappeared. Today's tables welcome a palette of colors and textures, the sophisticated rainbow of a collection of pastels — and a host or hostess with an eye to seeing the ordinary in extraordinary ways. Even an iron can be part of your creative repertoire. A plain dinner napkin takes on new interest of shape and shadow with a checkerboard series of squares pressed into the fabric. Remember that pressing hard-edged folds into the same linen can lead to rot along the creases, so rotate the napkins on which you use this technique.

the trousseau

Nowadays, when brides and grooms are just as likely to register at a sporting-goods store for sea-kayaking paraphernalia as they are to request silver, linens, and crystal, the trousseau has come to seem charmingly anachronistic. Although trousseaux date back hundreds of years, the heyday of the bridal trousseau — piles and piles of linens, lovingly stitched and monogrammed — was the 19th century. By then, the phenomenon of aristocratic young ladies heading off to the altar equipped with linen closets full of convent-sewn cloths had become far more egalitarian. Linens had moved from the realm of

the privileged to the "hope chests" of the bourgeoisie. Elegant department stores that offered "trousseau" counters for eager shoppers to browse January white sales, and catalogs that featured hand-glued swatches of cloth, all contributed to a fever of acquisition. Still, despite the commercial aspects of the purchased trousseau, the preferred color — white — continued to imbue linen with an aura of purity. In 1854, as part of the ritual surrounding the Immaculate Conception, Pope Pius IX established the Virgin Mary as the patron saint of linen maids. ◞

purity

caretaking

Part of the pleasure of linen comes from the texture and feel of very fine cloth. And yet, it is that very fineness that sometimes dissuades people from collecting and using beautiful fabrics. The beauty of a napkin can come from the sumptuous fabric itself, perhaps a delicate circle of silk that visually and tactilely creates a waterfall when tucked casually, gently into a goblet. With today's washable fabrics, silk napkins aren't as indulgent as they might seem. But, like all good fabrics, they require some special care. A few trade secrets in storing silk or linen: Never store linens with spots. You're inviting moths and other creepy-crawlies. Always store linens gently folded or rolled. Don't press

hard-edged folds into linen.
This can lead to fabric rot
along the creases. Do store
vintage linens in acid-free
paper. This offers protection
against aging and yellowing.
Do consider storing a lavender
or dried rose-petal sachet
with your linens. (If you're
using rose petals, make sure
you dry them in the shade,
then mix with dry lemon peel
in a 2-1 ratio with the flower
petals.) You can make your own
no-sew sachet simply by gathering and drying the flower
heads, filling a linen handkerchief, and tying them up
with a ribbon. A gentle peri-
odic squeeze to the sachet will
rerelease the fragrance. ❧

whitening

Collecting and using vintage linens is such a pleasure. Should you pass up a great find if it's yellowed? Not necessarily. Most linens can be whitened with a little time and effort. First, soak the piece overnight in plain, room-temperature water, simply to remove lingering dirt or soap. Then, soak in a highly diluted solution of non-chlorine bleach (one-half cup of dry oxygen bleach to two or three gallons of water). Finally, wash in a tub of hot water and mild soap. Rinse thoroughly, then roll the linen in a clean towel to soak up the extra water. Never wring or twist wet linen; it can tear or split easily. Spread flat to dry.

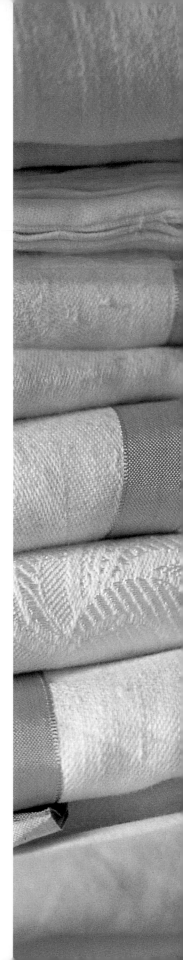

Linens that are used and enjoyed cannot

escape the misadventures of daily life — spots,

spills, candle wax, lipstick. Different

stains call for different treatments — and,

of course, all stains should be tended

to before the entire piece is laundered.

Berries, fruit, and red wine should be

sprinkled with salt and left to sit for a

few hours in cold water. Rinse well.

For grease stains, mix a paste of baking

soda, mild detergent, and oxygen bleach.

For candle wax, run an ice cube over the spot

until it's completely hardened, then

flake it off the fabric. Then, put the cloth

between sheets of clean brown paper

or paper towel and press with a warm iron,

moving the paper continuously until

the wax is absorbed. Wax and dye combine in

lipstick — and require special treatment.

Try warm water and soap first, then escalate

to sponging with 70% isopropyl alcohol

(or a dry cleaning solvent), and finally

to a weak nonchlorine bleach solution.

To remove a resistant stain from a sturdy

fabric, stretch the cloth over a bucket

and pour boiling water directly from the

kettle. Repeat until the stain disappears,

put the whole cloth in the bucket, and

let it soak in a mild soap. A little

effort, and your linens are restored to

their pristine state. ⌒

Antique stores, linen markets, tag and garage sales, even liquidation sales for hotels and restaurants can turn up wonderful treasures. From traditional French country brocante markets to Mid-western church rummage sales, there are finds for those with a good eye and a little patience. When you're shopping for old

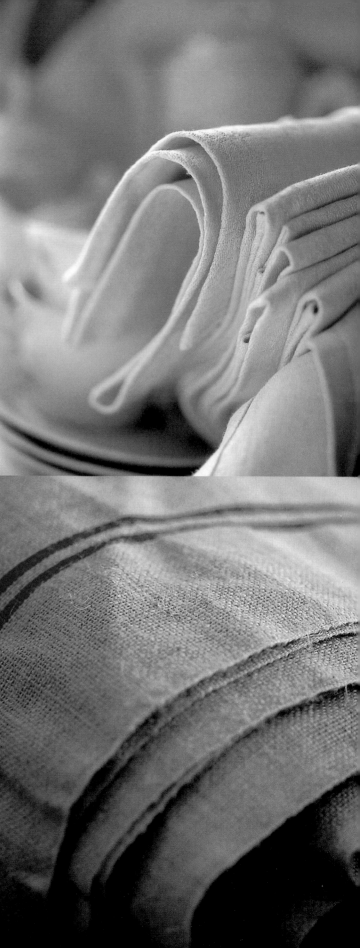

and fall apart over time. If it smells dusty, this may be a sign of dryness, and an early warning that the fabric may split. Linen in good condition shouldn't sound crisp or crinkly to the touch. If it does, that's evidence the fabric may have dried out, lost its suppleness, and become very brittle. Crush a handful and listen!

linens, don't be put off by yellowed color. Most linens can be whitened (see pages 22-23). Old, set stains are much more difficult to remove. The condition of the cloth is very important. Bring it up to your nose and breathe deeply. If there's a strong smell of bleach, it may mean it was never rinsed away, and the fibers will weaken

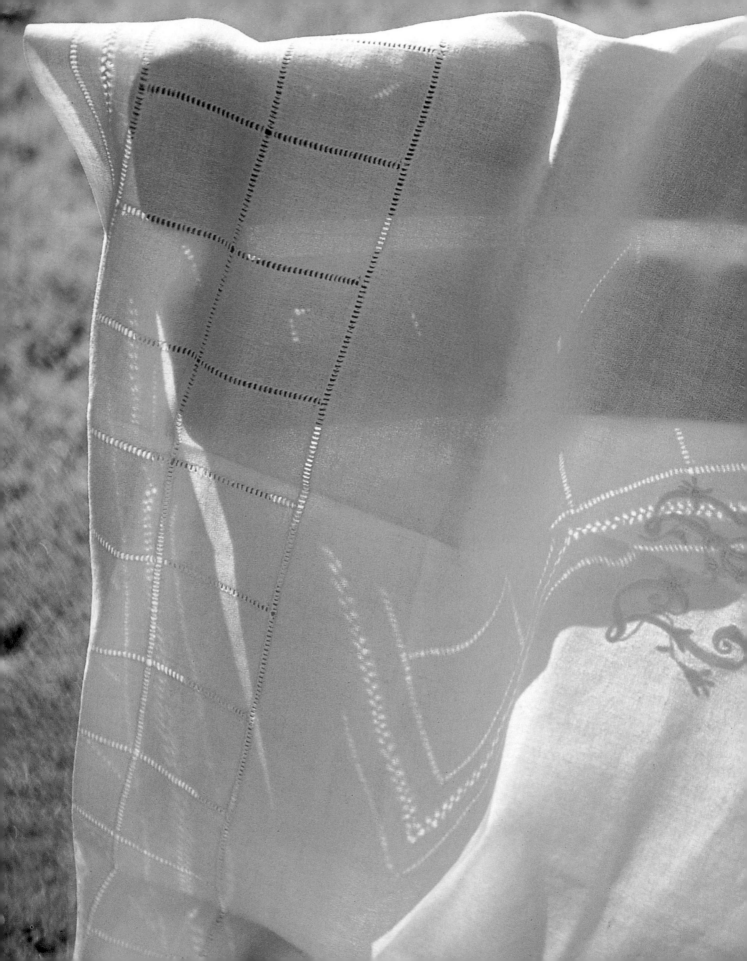

decoration

Linen has its own decorative vocabulary. There are
dozens of ornamental lace styles, including applique;
Battenberg, named in honor of members of Queen Victoria's
family who married into the German Battenberg family;
crocheted; and the delicate *punto in aria*, "stitches
in air," created with needle and thread on a mesh
background. In addition, there are elegant borders
such as *broderie anglaise* or eyelet, an embroidery-
like technique that creates oval or circular holes
with tiny stitches and fagoting; an open-work ornament,
created by pulling out horizontal threads and tying
the remaining vertical threads into hourglass-shaped
groups. The look of such ornamented linen is so rich
and beautifully textured, it's difficult to believe
the artistry is accomplished with nothing more than
needle, thread, fine fabric, patience, and skill.

monograms

Monograms, so elegant, so traditional, and so optimistic (they symbolize, after all, a community's confidence in the permanence of a marriage) have neither romantic nor decorative origins. In the Middle Ages, linens were marked simply so they could be identified. The embroidered monogram reached its height in the 19th century, in imitation of royally marked linens. When Grace Kelly became Princess Grace, she had her favorite flowers — blue hydrangeas — embroidered on her monogrammed linens. Today, whether executed by hand in a simple chain stitch or a more elaborate Beauvais — or even by machine — monogrammed linen napkins take on a timeless, heirloom quality. ⌒

It's no mystery why vintage and antique linens have become such contemporary collectibles. In a sense, their character only begins to reveal itself as the years go by. Part of the great tactile pleasure of linen napkins certainly comes with age. As napkins are used and laundered, the fabric grows softer and softer over time. Laundered, unstarched, gently ironed, and folded at table, napkins take on a worn grace. Little wonder that frayed table linens were once recycled into baby clothes and bandages. They offer their own soft welcome.

patterns

Part of the pleasure of treating the table
as a blank canvas — and the elements of
the table as your palette — is the world
of possibilities that opens up. A simple
white organdy napkin enhanced with tiny
balls is counterpointed with a beaded
plate and the delicately etched circles

on the elegant flute. Damask napkins
woven with a tracery of fruit could be
echoed subtly with a china pattern or
even a still-life centerpiece of seasonal,
summer fruits. A dining table with in-
laid squares of wood invites the use of
checkerboard napkins. Finding and com-
bining subtle patterns and themes in your
own collection of table elements can be
a tribute to your artistic eye, and give
a fresh look and feel to the table. ⌒

warm

The origins of the word *armoire* are surprisingly nondomestic. The word comes from the Latin *armarium* by way of the Old French *aumoire*, designating a chest for storing arms. It's not clear exactly when the word changed meaning, but it's quite heartening to think of it symbolizing the passage from war to peacetime, when families could afford to count linens rather than weapons as household assets. And, in fact, the warm sight (and fragrance) of a well-ordered linen cupboard — with table, bath, and bed linens neatly folded on lavender-scented paper — does feel like something of a defense against the chaos and unpredictability of the outside world. ⌇⌇⌇⌇

St. Paul wasn't the only one who had a transforming experience on the road to Damascus. Europeans began using damask cloths on

their tables in the Middle Ages, when the Crusaders, returning from Damascus, brought back samples of the beautiful fabrics they

found there. True damask can be woven of linen, silk, cotton, or wool, and carries a lovely subtle pattern that is entirely reversible.

the case for cloth

"Indeed it ought to be a cardinal rule in every home that the silver, linen, and fine manners are to be used every day. Use brightens and whitens all three and does not wear them anything like so much as lying in wait for company," wrote Emily Holt in *The Complete Housekeeper*. Table linens, soft with age, or starched to a fare-thee-well for a dinner party, are wonderful everyday indulgences. Hung to dry in the sun so they are sweet-smelling or finger-pressed when slightly damp, linens are one of the friendliest, most ecological and affordable of life's little luxuries. In fact, paper napkins have neither attractiveness nor economy to recommend them. They add to paper waste and they don't stand up particularly well to the rigors of a pleasantly messy barbecued sparerib or crab dinner. ⌒

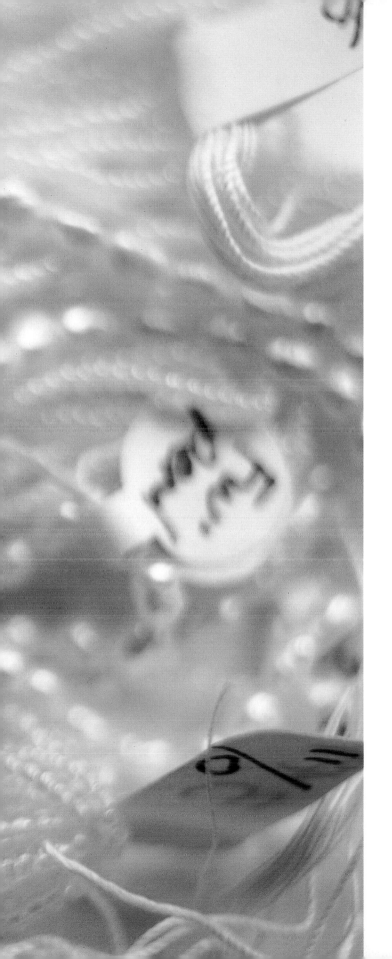

enhanced

Enhancing linens requires little more than an open mind, an artful eye, and a bit of time. In this chapter, we explore ways to add whimsy, ornamentation, and a myriad of special touches to table linens. None of the ideas require great time or skill. Most depend on seeing table linens as simply an extension of the creativity, visual style, and willingness to try something new that already guides your approach to creating warm and welcoming environments. You'll find ideas on party favors, new ways to exploit that old standby, the button box, and a fresh approach or two to folding napkins. Since linens need some special care to look their best, you'll also find additional information on laundering for best results. Most of all, you should be inspired to find your own special ways to add something — a single blossom, a twist of ribbon, a collection of charms — that enhances your individual style. ◇◇◇◇◇

adaptability

Handsome fabric is handsome fabric.
So, one of the pleasures of collecting
and using linens is that a piece originally intended for one use can grace-
fully be put to another. Drape canvas
painters' cloths on an oversized dining
table. Overlap embroidered tea napkins
down the center of a table for a runner. Or, try linen handkerchiefs as a
substitute for tea napkins themselves.
The delicacy of the handkerchief linen
echoes the fragile beauty of spring's
first grape hyacinths. Since the pur-
pose of a napkin is both decorative and
functional, any cloth that meets both
criteria can be pressed into service. ∽

sherry and walnuts and...crackers by the dessert spoons."

"Mistletoe hung from the gas brackets in all the front parlours; there was

Dylan Thomas, *A Child's Christmas in Wales*

Nowadays, "party favors" seem restricted

to one of two places — the children's

birthday party and the grand charity event.

But the idea of favors — little tokens

of affection from host to guest — is a uni-

versally engaging one. Who doesn't like

the surprise of an unexpected treat at

the table? The holidays create a perfect

excuse for giving party favors — lay

an ornament, a piece of gold-foil-wrapped

Hanukkah gelt, or a decadent chocolate

Santa, on crisply pressed napkins and your

table takes on a seasonal tone. You can

even vary the favors as you go around the

table, tailoring them to your guest's

taste and interests — Christmas crackers,

ribbon-tied cookie cutters, a sachet of

holiday potpourri.

buttons

Simple napkins beg for transformation. Many people keep

button boxes or tins, repositories for buttons that are

unusual, beautiful, or have sentimental value. And if

you don't, interesting buttons are available everywhere

from fabric, jewelry, and antique stores to flea markets

and costume shops. Consider tiny pearl buttons on cream

linen, elegant covered buttons on damask, carved wooden

or brass buttons on cotton. A whimsical collection of

different buttons adds texture and interest to a straightfor-

ward napkin. If the buttons are antique, test their

launderability before sewing them on to good linens. ⌢

How to... add drama and interest to linens with the simplest of resources and a measure of creativity. A few minutes with a needle and thread and you can enhance a napkin with interesting buttons, charms, or beads. Distinctive rubber stamps and a pad of washable ink create

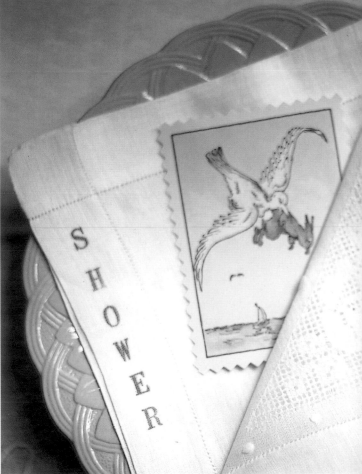

the opportunity to customize linens. Stamp "shower" or the baby's name on a cotton napkin for a very special look. The tiny guest of honor may even take the napkins home. Use washable fabric paint to create your own mini-landscape, an abstract pattern, a scattering of

impressionistic flowers. Or consider the fine art of folding, which creates an empty pocket ready to hold a surprise for each guest. The surprise can be thematic — a tea bag or silver tea ball for an afternoon tea, a packet of flower seeds for a spring luncheon, a vintage

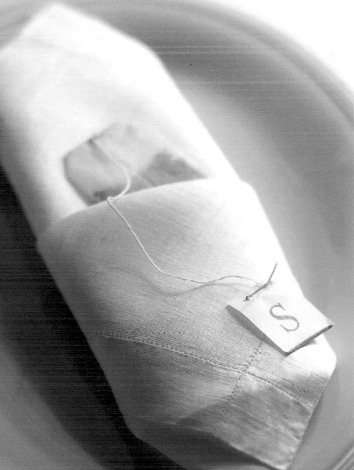

postcard for a bon voyage dinner. Sumptuous fabric, made even more elegant with a rococo tassel and nestled in a clear bowl, drapes beautifully at a place setting. Fabric ornaments — from fringe to silk flowers — are easy to attach to a single corner for an impact, with little effort.

luxury

There's an entire repertoire
of elaborate napkin folds —
from the classic Princess to
the stately, mitred Bishop's
Hat to the elaborately cascad-
ing Peacock, which features an
accordion-pleated and draped
"tail" tumbling over the side
of a stemmed wineglass. For
today's warmer, less regimented

53

entertaining climate, softer,
more creative folds seem just
right. A luxurious damask napkin is gently arranged and
ribbon-tied to mimic the drape
of a woman's scarf. It can also
be secured at the bottom with a
decorative pin or simply marked
with a single blossom. ✑

glamour

54 The sparkle of crystal flutes, gleaming on silver, is echoed by the glazed, ornamental acorns tied as accents on crisply starched napkins. It's a quietly glittering look for a candlelit evening. Or, try tying napkins in metallic ribbon, or encircle them in a band of gold leaf paper. Gather two napkins, in dramatically contrasting colors, in an heirloom silver napkin ring. Use fabric paint or metallic ink to write glittering, evocative words on the tablecloth — bon voyage, it's twins!, golden anniversary. Paint the edges of simple napkins with gold fabric paint. ⌣

more is more

Once upon a time, the mother of the
bride had the pleasant duty of "display-
ing" the engaged couple's wedding
gifts for friends and family to see.
A room was cleared, a long table set
up covered with linen, and the extrava-
ganza laid out — from soup (bowls) to
nut (dishes). Although the custom has
faded, there is something wonderful
and sumptuous about seeing a lovely
collection of linen — not tucked away
in a closet or hope chest — but beautifully layered fingertip towels
on bread cloths on creamy tablecloths.
The varying shades of linen — from
rosy damasks to pure white linen
to tea-dipped antique lace trims — make
a glowing palette. ⌒

celebrations

In the pantheon of traditional remembrances for anniversaries — paper for the first, silver for the twenty-fifth, gold for the fiftieth — linen holds a very special spot. Linen is the traditional gift for the twelfth anniversary (and its companion, lace, is designated for the thirteenth). A dozen years seems like a wonderful accomplishment. The newlywed years are gone; if there are children, they're still likely to be young, and the leisure of retirement is far, far away. How better to celebrate than with an extravagant bottle of champagne and twelve ribbon-tied cocktail napkins? To life, to love, to the next dozen years — and the dozen after that! ⌒

private lives of ghosts and archbishops and such."

"We used to sit there at the table after the noon dinner or on Sundays, and talk about the

M.F.K. Fisher, *Long Ago in France*

Textiles must be the most

mutable of art materials.

Soft and damp, fresh from

the laundry, linen napkins

can be transformed into

substantive sculpture with

a little starch, an iron,

and a few skillful folds.

The Princess is one of the

most classic folds — elegant

without being fussy, fanned

and placed center stage

on the plate, ready to be

uncreated with a flick of

the wrist and put to rest

on a guest's lap. ⌒

fanciful tables

At 17th-century tables, it was not unusual
to see heavily starched napkins transformed
into rigged sailing ships, Spanish fans, or
fanciful castles. The table was a place for
fantasy, whimsy, indulgence. Today, we can
carry out that sentiment by seeing linens as
the backdrop for the sheer theater of the
table. Heap seashells in the center of the
table to set the stage for a beach vaca-
tion. Tuck a little foreign currency into
each napkin to signal the cuisine theme for
the evening. Sew tiny heart charms or rings
onto napkins to commemorate a special
anniversary. Thread kitchen string through
a fresh vegetable on the menu — pea pods,
fava beans, a wild mushroom, or a chili
pepper — and attach one to each napkin.

texture, light, color

"Art of the table" takes us back to the still-life painters who knew that domestic visual imagery can remind us of the richness of everyday life. Memorable tabletop beauty is composed of equal parts texture — linen, silver, china — and light. The lights and shadows cast by candles, late morning sun streaming through a window, or gently dimmed lights from an overhead chandelier shape and sculpt what we experience at the table. A napkin lovingly enhanced with beads, a monogram that honors a family — these all elevate the commonplace to something quite special. Napkins made of elegant fabrics — heavy linens, polished cottons, richly colored silks — create a sense of "special occasion."

Silk napkins in shades of sweet summer melons — cantaloupe, honeydew, Crenshaw. Spilling out of a silver compote, they illustrate how three elements — color, texture, and presentation — combine to create a memorable visual effect. In an era of fast food and meals on the run, taking time to create a beautiful environment, appreciating and enhancing all the elements of the table — from pearls on a napkin to a sprig of basil on fresh tomatoes — is a special gift. "The table is a meeting place," wrote Laurie Colwin in *More Home Cooking*, "a gathering ground, the source of sustenance and nourishment, festivity, safety, and satisfaction. A person cooking is a person giving: Even the simplest food is a gift." And a meal served on a table created with care is a symbol of a particularly generous heart.

placed

Just before the doorbell rings or just before the family comes drifting into the dining room, you take a last look around. No matter how simply you've set the table, you've created an environment, an environment that signals what kind of gathering this is going to be. Part of the secret of enjoying everyday life is taking pleasure in the qualities that surround our tables. And,

whether that table is mahogany in the dining room, scrubbed pine in the kitchen, a funky formica in front of the VCR, a wicker tray in the bedroom, or a redwood trestle under a tree, the linens you put in place give a character to the event and the meal you share. In this chapter, we explore linens in their environment, waiting for you, waiting for friends and family — and communicating a very clear sense of occasion.

after dark

In a room lit by candles, dim lamps, and a full moon pouring in the window, an après-theater party can take on special drama. Heavy jet-black napkins, which might look somber on a dining table, add luster and romance to a sideboard set with fruit, cheeses, and indulgent treats. The sparkle from a tray of champagne glasses is reflected in the creamy marble serving pedestals and the shimmery, silvery ribbons that tie up the napkins. Deep colors — forest green, royal burgundy, rich coffee, ebony — convey a sense of luxurious abundance, perfect for a late-night gathering.

72

Thanks to the magic of the silver
screen, our collective romantic memories
are filled with grand scenes that
take place over a white-clothed table.

74

William Powell toasting Myrna Loy

in *The Thin Man*, high drama

when the Barrymores (John and Lionel),

are joined by Marie Dressler and

a luminous Jean Harlow for

Dinner at Eight, David Niven

and Deborah Kerr exchanging glances

at *Separate Tables* — and of course,

the art of the conversation,

as carried out by Andre Gregory and

Wallace Shawn in *My Dinner with Andre.*

simply silk

Truly sumptuous fabric needs no further adornment.
Fortuny silk napkins are loosely knotted to sit
as ripples of color on an exquisite plate. Or, consider
a simple napkin ring of silk or woven satin braid,
with the napkin gently drawn through and fanned on the
plate. Drapery or upholstery notion stores can be a
source for remarkably luxurious cording, used to tie
around an elegant napkin. Many silk napkins need to be
dry-cleaned, of course. However, the washable silk
fabrics make wonderful napkins, and require only a little more care than linen. Some can even be washed by
machine on a gentle cycle. Remember to turn silk on the
wrong side to iron, using a dry iron on a low setting
with a press cloth to protect the fabric. Like linen
(or any natural fabric) silk needs to breathe, so make
sure it's not stored away in airtight plastic. Loosely
wrapped tissue or acid-free paper works best of all.

perfect and radiantly beautiful."

"That afternoon the whole world seemed to devote itself to being

Frances Hodgson Burnett, *The Secret Garden*

omance

Sometimes the simplest
ideas create the most
romantic surprises. Dinner
à deux? Layered linens,
set on a table placed on
a balcony or terrace, blur
the boundary between
indoors and out-of-doors.
The serendipity of a
perfect summer fig leaf,
plucked from a tree and
pinned to the corner of a
soft cloth as a "found"
ornament. Any interestingly
shaped, large-scale leaf
or cluster of leaves —
sycamore, oak, tendrils
of ivy — will do. ∽

modern classics

For people who grew up in the fifties and sixties, the wonderful clean lines of International style look just like home — our parents' home. There was great variety there, from witty deco on one end to the classic lines of Moderne on the other. Both translate into the saturated colors we see in sunset and chartreuse-colored linens and, of course, Fiestaware, Bauerware, and their uptown cousin, Russel Wright. It may be a tribute to the classicism of this look that the unapologetically colorful linens look so up-to-the-minute. Add a table runner, hand-painted in contemporary shapes and tones, and you have a perfect setting for a lighthearted evening. ⌒

Let yourself go! Set the table with wild abandon. Mix patterns of china by layering salad, dinner, charger differently at each place. Mix patterns of silver and crystal. And of course, use a differ-ent napkin and a different fold at each place. Just to make sure you have the right base for all this free-form creativity, consider creating a white-and-gold painted linen checkerboard to cover the entire table. As long as you're working in the same families of color, you'll create a series of one-of-a-kind place settings that harmonize splendidly.

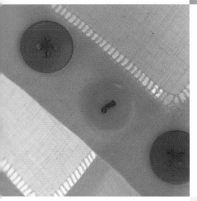

"A bright idea came into Alice's head. 'Is that the reason so many tea-things are put out here?' she asked. 'Yes, that's it,' said the Hatter with a sigh: 'it's always tea-time, and

we've no time to wash the things between whiles.' 'Then you keep moving round, I suppose?' said Alice. 'Exactly so,' said the Hatter." Lewis Carroll, *Alice in Wonderland*

egance

Both cloths and napkins are
delightful examples of form far
exceeding function. After all,
both were developed to serve
very practical purposes. Table-
cloths evolved to protect the
surface of the table, napkins to
protect clothing. But paying
attention to the beauty of the
cloth, to a special napkin fold,
or a wonderful collection of
napkin rings, adds a new and
very tactile dimension to the
table. Whether you're tying napkins up with wired silk ribbon
or homely raffia or a cut length
of English ivy, you're communicating a certain sense of style
that says you care about what
happens at the table. ∿∿∿

Linens are everyday treasures, reminders of all we have

to celebrate. As the traditional toast goes, "Health to

our bodies, peace to our minds, and plenty to our table."

napkin folds

the fan

rio

88 Think of folded napkins as a little sculpture for each guest. Here are six simple and elegant napkin folds to try, and a few rules of thumb: not all napkins are suited to all folds – the weight, stiffness, and pattern design of your napkin will determine which folds are going to work. There will be a bit of trial and error while you find a match between fold and napkin, and between folded napkin and place setting.

1. Fold napkin in half, take one of the short edges and fold toward and past center in one-inch accordion pleats until you have about four to five inches left at opposite end.

2. Holding the folds in place, fold the napkin in half through the center of the folds with the pleats on the outside.

3. Holding the pleated edge in your left hand, with pleat edges on top, take the top, right unfolded corner and bring it diagonally toward the bottom left and tuck into the folded edge, to support the napkin.

4. Place folded pleat edge toward you with finished edges left and begin to unfold the fan by gently pulling the pleats toward left until fan is in position.

1. Fold napkin in corners with four points at bottom.

2. Bring the top two layers up to meet the top point.

3. Bring the third layer up to approximately an inch from the top and follow with the last layer to approximately one inch from the last layer.

4. Fold right and left sides under the napkin forming either straight or tapered sides.

the orchid

1. Fold the napkin in half. Place fold at bottom edge. Bring upper left corner down to bottom center edge. Repeat with the right corner.

2. Bring bottom left point up to top center and repeat with the right bottom point. You should have a diamond shape with a center vertical fold.

3. At the top of the diamond shape, fold the points of the left and right sides back on themselves to form points that break the edge of the diamond.

4. Gather the bottom few inches of napkin with a napkin ring or ribbon.

french scarf

1. Fold napkin in half diagonally so that point is toward you.

2. With both hands and in one motion, hold napkin on top edge and begin to roll top edge away and under while bringing points down toward bottom point.

3. Gather the two points together and gather with a ribbon or a circle of herbs from the garden.

pure and simple

1. Fold napkin in half diagonally with straight edge toward you. Bring left and right corners up to meet at top point.

2. Turn napkin over and bring the lower corner up about three to five inches.

3. Bring left- and right-hand corners back underneath napkin at a slight diagonal so that the napkin tapers in toward bottom and creates elegant oval opening.

the princess

This is a very difficult fold to master, but the result is worth the effort.

1. Fold napkin in half and make a crease in the center line, then open napkin up again. Working lengthwise, fold the top half of the napkin into three parts by taking the top edge in toward the center line and then folding it back on itself, so that the top finished edge remains at the top, with a fold at the center line. Follow same instructions with second half.

2. Now, fold the napkin lengthwise in half so that the top half folds underneath the bottom. You should now have three folds on one side and two folds and two finished edges on the other.

3. Working lengthwise, mark the center of the napkin with your finger and fold the right-hand side in toward the center in a three fold so that the finished edges are still on the right edge and there is a fold at the center line. Repeat with the left side. It should now appear that you have two square-shaped folds with a center line.

4. Bring the first layer top left-hand corner across the center to the top right-hand corner, creating a triangle shape in the center. Press down on each crease to hold in place and continue to do so for each new triangle shape. Repeat with remaining left-hand corners and then repeat on the right side, being sure to bring up the remaining center points to the top center of fold. Ease the folds open, placing the center point toward your guest.

resources

California

**Chelsea Passage
at Barney's New York**
9570 Wilshire Blvd.
Los Angeles, CA 90212
310.276.4400

Fillamento
2185 Fillmore Street
San Francisco, CA 94115
415.931.2224

The Gardener
1836 Fourth Street
Berkeley, CA 94710
510.548.4545

Gump's
135 Post Street
San Francisco, CA 94108
415.984.1616

Brian Jeffries
7556 Melrose Avenue
Los Angeles, CA 90403
213.651.2539

Kisetsu
310 Sir Francis Drake Blvd.
San Anselmo, CA 94960
415.456.9070

Lacis
2982 Adeline St.
Berkeley, CA 94703
510.843.7290

Malibu Colony Co.
3835 Cross Creek
Malibu, CA 90265
310.317.0177

Nest
2300 Fillmore Street
San Francisco, CA 94115
415.292.6199

Pierre Deux
120 Maiden Lane
San Francisco, CA 94108
415.296.9940
for locations nationwide call:
415.383.0847

Pottery Barn
2100 Chestnut Street
San Francisco, CA 94123
415.441.1787
for locations nationwide call:
800.922-9934

Pullman & Co.
108 Throckmorton Ave.
Mill Valley, CA 94941

RH
2506 Sacramento,
San Francisco, CA 94115
415.346.1460

Room with a View
1600 Montana Avenue
Santa Monica, CA 90403
310.998.5858

Sue Fisher King
3067 Sacramento St.
San Francisco, CA 94115
415.922.9241

**Sue Fisher King
at Wilkes Bashford**
375 Sutter Street
San Francisco, CA 94108
415.986.4380

Summerhouse
21 Throckmorton
Mill Valley, CA 94941
415.383.6695

Sur la Table
1806 4th Street
Berkeley, CA 94710
510.849.2252

Tail of the Yak
2632 Ashby Ave.
Berkeley, CA 94705
510.841.9891

Vanderbuilt & Co.
71 Stanford Shopping Center
Palo Alto, CA 94304
415.324.1010

Vanderbuilt & Co.
1429 Main Street
St. Helena, CA 94574
707.963.1010

Versailles
1415 S. La Cienega Blvd.
Los Angeles, CA 90034
310.289.0392

Williams-Sonoma
150 Post Street
San Francisco, CA 94108
415.362.6904
for locations nationwide call:
800.541.1262

Z Gallerie
2071 Union Street
San Francisco, CA 94123
415.346.9000
for other locations call:
310.410.6650

Ampersand
5034 France Ave. South
Edina, MN 55410
612.920.2118

Branca Boutique
944 N. Rush St.
Chicago, Il 60611
312.664.4200

Elements
102 East Oak Street
Chicago, Il 60611
312.642.6574

Five Swans
309 East Lake Street
Wayzata, MN 55391
612.473.4685

Material Possessions
54 East Chestnut St.
Chicago, Il 60613
312.280.4885

Provisions
320 Water Street
Excelsior, MN 55331
612.474.6953

Tabula Tua
1015 W. Armitage
Chicago, Il 60614
312.525.3500

Crate and Barrel
646 N. Michigan Avenue
Chicago, Il 60611
312.787.5900
for locations nationwide call:
800.451.8217

Peppercorn
1235 Pearl Street
Boulder, CO 80302
303.449.5847

Squisito
2628 E. 3rd Avenue
Denver, CO 80206
303.331.8080

Spoons and Spice
4700 South 900 East
Salt Lake City, UT 84117
801.263.1898

Crossroads
27 East Main
Bozeman, MT 59715
406.587.2702

The Sideboard
425 Park Avenue
Idaho Falls, ID 83402
208.524.4228

ABC Carpet & Home
888 Broadway
New York, NY 10003
212.473.3000

Ad Hoc Housewares
410 West Broadway
New York, NY 10012
212.925.2652

Alice's Underground
481 Broadway
New York, NY 10012
212.431.9067

Aventura
65 Second Avenue
New York, NY 10024
212.769.2510

Chelsea Passage
at Barney's New York
660 Madison Avenue
New York, NY 10019
212.339.7300

Dean & Deluca
560 Broadway
New York, NY 10012
800.221.7714

Frank McIntosh
at Henri Bendel
712 Fifth Avenue
New York, NY 10019
212.247.1100

Bergdorf Goodman
754 Fifth Avenue
New York, NY 10019
212.753.7300

Felissimo
10 West 56th Street
New York, NY 10019
212.956.4438

Interieurs
114 Wooster Street
New York, NY 10012
212.343.0800

Simon Pearce
120 Wooster Street
New York, NY 10014
212.334.2390
contact store for locations
outside New York

Simon Pearce
500 Park Avenue
New York, NY 10022
212.421.8801

Portico Home
397 West Broadway
New York, NY 10012
212.941.780

Takashimaya
693 Fifth Avenue
New York, NY 10022
800.753.2038

Troy
138 Green Street
New York, NY 10012
212.941.4777

Wolfman-Gold &
Good Company
117 Mercer Street
New York, NY 10012
212.431.1888

Zona
97 Green Street
New York, NY 10012
212.925.6750

April Cornell
97 Church Street
Burlington, VT 05401
802.862.8211

Carol O'Neal
Antique Linens
P.O. Box 2171
Sag Harbor, NY 11963
516.725.9893

Grasshopper Shop
124 Main Street
Ellsworth, ME 04605
207.667.5816

Kimball Shop
Main Street
Northeast Harbor, ME 04662
207.276.3330

Linens of the Hill
52 Charles Street
Boston, MA 02114
617.227.1255

Pierre Deux
111 Newberry Street
Boston, MA 02116
617.536.6364
call for other
nationwide locations

Pacific Northwest

The Bon Marche
3rd and Pine St.
Seattle, WA 98181
206.506.6000

Domaine
661 120th Ave. NE
Bellevue, WA 98005
206.450.9900

Kitchen Kaboodle
404 N.W. Flanders
Portland, OR 97210
503.241.4040
call for other
Portland locations

The Kobos Company
2355 N.W. Vaughn
Portland, OR 97210
503.222.2181
call for other
Oregon locations

Larry's Market
100 Mercer Street
Seattle, WA 98109
206.213.0778

Sur la Table
84 Pine Street
Seattle, WA 98101
206.448.2244

Table Top Shop
2664 NE University
Village Court
Seattle, WA 98105
206.526.8480

Trivia
355 NW Gilman Blvd.
Issaquah, WA 98027
206.392.5180

South

Jay Aronson
200 Broadway, Suite #132
New Orleans, LA 70118
504.865.1186

Custom Linens
3068 College Drive
Baton Rouge, LA 70808
504.924.0994

Berings
6102 Westheimer
Houston, TX 77057
713.785.6400

Events
1966 West Gray
Houston, TX 77019
713.520.5700

Fast Buck Freddie's
500 Duvall Street
Key West, FL 33040-6553
305.294.2007

Stanley Korshak
500 Crescent Ct. Suite 100
Dallas, TX 75201
214.871.3600

Longoria Collection
6524 Woodway
Houston, TX 77057
713.467.8495

Maddix Deluxe
1034 N. Highland Avenue
Atlanta, GA 30306
404.892.9337

Neiman Marcus
1618 Main Street
Dallas, TX 75201
214.741.6911
call for other
nationwide locations

Peridot
514 East Paces Ferry Road
Atlanta, GA 30305
404.261.7028

Translations
4014 Villanova
Dallas, TX 75225
214.373.8391

Many of the beautiful
elements of the table seen
in this book come from
the stores below:

Gump's
135 Post Street,
San Francisco, CA
Phone: 415.982.1616
Pages: Cover, 60, 67 (silver
compote), 81 (tablerunner),
83 (linen & china)

Fillamento
2185 Fillmore Street,
San Francisco, CA
Phone: 415.931.2224
Pages: 15, 19, 20, 63, 67
(napkins), 76 (napkin),
81 (candlesticks), 88

Sue Fisher King
3067 Sacramento Street,
San Francisco, CA
Phone: 415.922.7276
Pages: 13, 55 (napkins), 59

Randolph & Hein, Inc.
101 Henry Adams,
San Francisco, CA
Phone: 415.346.1460
Pages: 72 & 73 (fabrics)

Dishes Delmar
1359 Waller,
San Francisco, CA
Phone: 415.558.8882
Pages: 80, 81 (plates,
glassware, flatware,
& pottery)

Fuchsia Dentelles
2 Rue Ave Maria,
Paris, 75004 France
Phone: 48.04.75.61
Pages: 4, 6, 22, 24, 25,
26, 27, 38, 39

93

acknowledgments:

It is a pleasure to express our deep gratitude and appreciation to the following people, whose generosity, support, and creativity contributed so enormously to this book. And so we acknowledge:

~ Jenny Barry, who created this series and gave us the opportunity to produce it.

~ Jennifer Morla, Petra Geiger, and the staff at Morla Design for giving the photos and words form, spirit, and style.

~ Linda Peterson for her glowing words that married photography and design, and who told this story with knowledge, poetry, humor, and grace.

~ Jennifer Ward, Maura Carey Damacion, and the staff at Collins Publishers San Francisco for their trust, enthusiasm, and support.

~ Sandra Cook for food styled with simplicity and elegance, and for her continued encouragement of this project.

~ K.D. Sullivan for great and swift copyediting.

~ Jeri Jones, photo assistant extraordinaire, for her diligence and gracious spirit.

We were also fortunate to have wonderful locations
to photograph and we want to thank the following
people for their hospitality, generosity, and style:

Randolph Arczynski, Burt Tessler, Jimmy Wentworth,
Jennifer Morla, and Nilus de Matran.

Many of the beautiful things photographed in this
book were generously loaned to us and we are delighted
to thank: Shirley Wilson and Gump's; Iris Fuller and
the staff at Fillamento; Sue Fisher King and her
staff; Randolph Arczynski of Randolph and Hein, Inc.;
F. Dorian; Madame Casas at Fuchsia Dentelle, Paris;
and Burt Tessler at Dishes Delmar. Thank you, too,
to George DoLese for his generosity and kindness to
us in Paris.

This book was a labor of love and the loved ones who
supported us through this labor were: Mark Steisel,
Kate Slavin, Sybil Slavin, Lillian Moss, Hedy Green,
Isabel Fife, and the friends and family of
Donald Sheckler.

bibliography:

Child, Lydia M.F. The American Frugal Housewife, 20th edition, Harper & Row, 1972 (original edition 1836).

Clise, Michele Durkson. The Linen Closet: How to Care for Your Fine Linens and Lace, Chronicle Books, 1996.

de Bonneville, Francoise. The Book of Fine Linen, Flammarion, 1994.

Foley, Tricia. Linens and Lace, Clarkson Potter, 1990.

Hetzer, Linda. The Simple Art of Napkin Folding, Hearst Books, 1980.

Post, Elizabeth L. Emily Post's Etiquette, 14th edition, Harper & Row, 1984.

Smith, Susy, and Lansdown, Karen. The Creative Art of Table Decorations, Longmeadow Press, 1987.

Wallace, Dan (ed). The Natural Formula Book for Home & Yard, Rodale Press, 1982.

credits:

Grateful acknowledgment is made to Simon & Schuster for permission to reprint an excerpt from *Long Ago in France: The Years in Dijon* by M.F.K. Fisher. Copyright © 1991 by M.F.K. Fisher. Reprinted by permission of Simon & Schuster.

Grateful acknowledgment is made to Alfred A. Knopf for permission to reprint an excerpt from *More Home Cooking* by Laurie Colwin. Copyright © 1988. Reprinted by permission of Alfred A. Knopf.

We were also fortunate to have wonderful locations
to photograph and we want to thank the following
people for their hospitality, generosity, and style:

Randolph Arczynski, Burt Tessler, Jimmy Wentworth,
Jennifer Morla, and Nilus de Matran.

Many of the beautiful things photographed in this
book were generously loaned to us and we are delighted
to thank: Shirley Wilson and Gump's; Iris Fuller and
the staff at Fillamento; Sue Fisher King and her
staff; Randolph Arczynski of Randolph and Hein, Inc.;
F. Dorian; Madame Casas at Fuchsia Dentelle, Paris;
and Burt Tessler at Dishes Delmar. Thank you, too,
to George DoLese for his generosity and kindness to
us in Paris.

This book was a labor of love and the loved ones who
supported us through this labor were: Mark Steisel,
Kate Slavin, Sybil Slavin, Lillian Moss, Hedy Green,
Isabel Fife, and the friends and family of
Donald Sheckler.

bibliography:

Child, Lydia M.F. <u>The American Frugal Housewife</u>, 20th edition, Harper & Row, 1972 (original edition 1836).

Clise, Michele Durkson. <u>The Linen Closet: How to Care for Your Fine Linens and Lace</u>, Chronicle Books, 1996.

de Bonneville, Francoise. <u>The Book of Fine Linen</u>, Flammarion, 1994.

Foley, Tricia. <u>Linens and Lace</u>, Clarkson Potter, 1990.

Hetzer, Linda. <u>The Simple Art of Napkin Folding</u>, Hearst Books, 1980.

Post, Elizabeth L. <u>Emily Post's Etiquette</u>, 14th edition, Harper & Row, 1984.

Smith, Susy, and Lansdown, Karen. <u>The Creative Art of Table Decorations</u>, Longmeadow Press, 1987.

Wallace, Dan (ed). <u>The Natural Formula Book for Home & Yard</u>, Rodale Press, 1982.

credits:

Grateful acknowledgment is made to Simon & Schuster for permission to reprint an excerpt from *Long Ago in France: The Years in Dijon* by M.F.K. Fisher. Copyright © 1991 by M.F.K. Fisher. Reprinted by permission of Simon & Schuster.

Grateful acknowledgment is made to Alfred A. Knopf for permission to reprint an excerpt from *More Home Cooking* by Laurie Colwin. Copyright © 1988. Reprinted by permission of Alfred A. Knopf.